LEVERAGE

Taking Advantage of your Right-Now

to Build your Tomorrow

By William Clark

Printed in the United States of America
First Printing, 2014
ISBN-13 978-0615947518

Willis Dawson Publishing House
PO Box 18886
Philadelphia, PA 19119

Christianity, Faith, and Personal Development.

Table of Contents

To my wife and children…
Thank you for your love and support.

To my parents…
I have what I have because of what you have poured into me.

To BCOGH Philly…
Your prayers and support will not be forgotten. I am grateful for each and every one of you!

Introduction

This book started as a sermon. A portion of this sermon addressed the difference between the haves and have-nots. Other portions of this sermon sought to drive significant thought toward the lack of the internal desire, for some in the African American community, to pursue meaningful life change. God sees all humans as the same, regardless of their skin color, national or continental origin, or even the manner in which a person arrived on these shores. However, study after study indicates that while the income gap between African Americans and Caucasian Americans has narrowed in the past two generations, the wealth gap, that is, the difference in the value of a family's assets has not narrowed. I wanted to inspire the congregants to assess their own potential for wealth building, and to launch themselves into a campaign of substantive life change.

To begin the book, I had to ask myself what holds people back from experiencing the change they desire. I discovered that there were at least three things that the average person can control that can work for or against them in the process of creating significant life change. First, people sell themselves short. They believe themselves unworthy, and therefore, they create no material worth. Second, their goals are misaligned with their authentic selves. They may want to provide an equal level of material goods for their families compared to their peers, but this is consumption, not wealth-building. Third, and this is most common, they have no idea how to value themselves and their skills. As a result, it becomes difficult for them to plan their path to financial independence.

I hope you are edified and strengthened by this book. You will learn how to change the three impediments to your success, but before you even learn practical tips, tools, and techniques, you will learn principles of leadership, including self-leadership, which is the judicious application of cognitive behavioral techniques to bring your internal state in line with the success you want to achieve. Once you have changed your internal conversation and created the conditions for success, including wealth building, you will learn how to launch your campaign for change from your current life position.

May God prosper your journey.

William Clark

One

Leverage Starts with Leadership

You want to achieve some sort of success – any sort of success – and you are wondering how. The key to the fulfillment of this desire may be found in how good of a leader you are. For some people, the answer to the next question is obvious, but it underlines most of our assumptions about leaders. "What does leadership have to do with becoming successful, particularly if success is defined as living a more prosperous life?" Leadership is properly defined as having the ability to influence others to achieve a goal. This is useful when you are leading a team. I would like to offer you a new way of looking at leadership and how leadership applies to you, the individual. The term self-leadership describes how one is capable of influencing himself or herself to achieve a specific goal, to achieve a specific way of thinking, and how to provide positive rewards to oneself for performing as expected. Self-leadership is a foundational tool in leveraging the assets you currently have to become successful. Let's evaluate self-leadership a little more.

There are three essential components to self-leadership. They include the following.

- Cognitive techniques: methods of thinking to achieve goal,
- Behavioral techniques: behavioral responses to achieve set goals,
- Natural rewards: rewarding self for meeting goals and performing well.

I am most concerned with how you think. This does not discount the value of behavioral techniques and the natural rewards we give ourselves for performing. However, I am asserting that after you prepare your mind to leverage what you have, you will understand how to put into action your new way of thinking to realize the difference you want to see in your life.

Cognitive techniques for self-leadership focus on visualizing success, effective self-talk, and evaluating beliefs and assumptions. Let's explore each area briefly.

Visualizing your success is probably one of the most recognizable of the cognitive behavioral techniques. Visualizing your success is simply envisioning yourself doing what you plan to do. Think about the pre-shot routine that a golfer goes through. He assesses the overall shot, visualizes the ball on the grass, sees the hitting zone on the ball, and takes a practice swing that he knows that, if he executes correctly, will put the golf ball in the target area. Then he steps up to the ball and brings his visualization into reality.

Can you see yourself successfully completing the task in front of you? Generally, we visualize ourselves completing a task before we actually do it. Often, you will find yourself seeing that vision as soon as the thought of completing a task comes to mind. It is amazing how fast our minds are able to view far in advance our success or failure. As quickly as we can see ourselves doing something successfully, we can see ourselves equally quickly not being successful. This quick glimpse into the future provides a parameter of action that can dictate our next steps. It is your thinking that can propel you to the next phase of your action plan, but at the same time, your thinking can hold you back from even getting started.

Self-talk is the process of talking yourself through the steps of executing your plan. Often, you will find yourself having to be your own cheerleader to aid in overcoming your challenges. Cheerleading will result in talking to yourself and encouraging yourself. Why does this happen? Perhaps, before we have the opportunity to share our thoughts and ideas with people around us, we are wise enough to spend the alone-time needed to know ourselves and what we would like to accomplish. The time alone with your ideas creates an atmosphere conducive for developing the right strategies to make your ideas a reality. There are too many people that do not think before they act and as a result, they have a lot of "woulda", "coulda", "shouldas". All of this can be avoided if these same people cultivate the habit of positive, goal-directed self-talk.

Evaluating your assumptions means determining the value of what you believe to be true and how those beliefs hold up during difficult times. We learn more about our belief systems when they are challenged. We learn if what we believe has substance or if it is all fluff. Do not be afraid that your belief system will fail you, coming unhinged when you face difficult times; rather, consider the idea that your beliefs will be strengthened by the act of confronting challenges. Difficult times will help you articulate your faith position and to learn how best to use it in every life situation.

I chose to have this brief conversation with you about self-leadership as a context to begin your journey of leverage. We all possess the power of leverage and are capable of releasing that power. A precondition to releasing this power is a solid knowledge of yourself and your capabilities. We tend to embrace life and its challenges based on our perspective, and sadly, the perspective many people have of themselves is inaccurate (usually, too negative) and causes them to do things that are not in their best interest. These off-base decisions are similar to injuring oneself with self-inflicted wounds. To be all you can be for yourself and for your family, you must focus directly and intentionally on your development. This builds a solid context for leveraging your assets for change.

Leverage is all about knowing what you possess and how to use it to realize change in your life. Leverage consists of three major components, which include asking for what you want, developing a plan to get to where you want to be, and finally executing the plan that you develop. In the subsequent pages of this book, you will be edified by the story of Jacob and how he leveraged what was available to him to change his life.

You will be exposed to ideas that will encourage you to reevaluate your use of your assets and how to best move forward from where you are today. Lastly, I believe you will be inspired to look at your situation differently and make choices that will snowball into a life that you can be proud of. Let's dig into Leverage.

Two

Ask For What You Want

Laying the right foundation

People do not receive what they want in life because either they do not ask for it or they do not know how to ask effectively. Asking for what you want is a part of experiencing abundance. Most people will suffer for long periods of time because they do not ask for the change they desire. Asking for what you want is central to creating change in your life. It is hard, if not impossible, to envision change in your life if you do not ask for it.

Asking for something does not guarantee you will receive it, but asking creates an awareness of your needs. This awareness builds a coalition of resources to help fulfill your needs. When you ask for what you want, you should be honest about what you are asking for. Dishonesty or disingenuousness in your asking can push away potential resources. The availability of resources, particularly during tough times, makes honesty an essential character trait. Without saying, honesty should be a part of who you are in times of need or abundance.

People stop short of asking for what they desire or need due to a self-imposed belief that their past disqualifies them or labels them as unworthy of asking. I struggled with this issue, like many of you who are reading this book. For a long time, I thought I was the only person who suffered loss in some of my investments due to my mistakes and lack of knowledge. As I matured out of these thoughts, I realized people who suffered the same fate preceded me, and there will be others that follow me that will make mistakes in the future.

In areas of life outside of business, some Christians have a propensity to impose upon themselves the notion that their past prevents them from experiencing the grace and blessings of God. They embrace the non-contextual meaning of John 9:31 when it says God does not hear a sinner's prayer, yet they quickly forget the premise that Christ was sent to forgive all sins. Jesus's sacrifice served to give everyone the chance to move beyond the sins that separate a sinner from a relationship with God. The intent of the scripture is to acknowledge that God does not respond to the special requests, prayers, or pleas of unrepentant sinners. He responds to those that worship and do His Will. You should be inspired to know that the moment you acknowledge your sin and become a sincere penitent, God is there to receive you. Thus, believers must get over the guilt that causes them to believe they are unqualified to ask God for grace and blessings. If you feel guilty for petitioning God, find out what it takes to please Him to remove your guilt. Asking God for the things you desire and need is normal but if you want to see those things come to pass, pleasing Him has to be your top priority.

Even if what you want from God is wisdom only, it can be difficult to bring yourself to ask Him for the intangible gift of wisdom because of the self-imposed thought that you are not worthy of His wisdom. These self-imposed thoughts may be a result of poor decision-making or ignoring God as chief consultant. The amazing thing about God is He has everything we desire and wants to give it to us in liberal measure. It is our selfish pursuits and desires that prevent us from asking God for the wisdom to overcome and deal with our issues. It is also the same reason why when we muster up the strength to ask God for wisdom, we often end up asking Him for the wrong thing.

The organization of our priorities creates a gap between sensible requests and selfishness. According to Proverbs 8, wisdom was present when God created the heavens and the earth. In the same chapter, the author describes wisdom and what it offers to people that take advantage of it. Within wisdom are riches and honor. Kings rule by wisdom. Wisdom causes its users to find favor with the Lord. These are just some of the benefits associated with seeking wisdom. Because God owns and controls wisdom, it is in our best interest to get used to asking God for this precious gift because it is a gift that He himself used to create the universe. If we are children of God, it makes sense to pursue and go after what our Father has to give to us for the asking.

The first step on your journey to self-sufficiency is education. The more you know about your goal, the more targeted your request will be of yourself, your intimates, your enterprise partners, or God. If you are not educated on what you are pursuing, you will find it extremely difficult to communicate your desires to people who are in position to help you. This advice goes beyond the realm of business and finances. You should educate yourself about the people with whom you are planning to enter into a relationship. It is best to know up front what you are getting yourself into before it is too late.

Everything we ask for should have a purpose and meaning behind it. As my parents used to say when I was growing up, "Do not try to keep up with the Joneses." Seriously, the idea of competing or keeping up, can ruin you and your family because you have not invested enough time learning who you are and what type of requests will make sense for the life you want to lead. The goal in life, especially if one wants to achieve success, is to know who you are as a person and why you are asking for specific things to advance your cause.

Whether you are asking for investors to invest in your business, a confirmation board to affirm your ministry, or you are asking the person you are dating to agree to marry you, your pursuit of these things requires clear authenticity and self-knowledge. Who are you and where are you going? If you want to determine if what you are asking God for is genuinely substantive toward your future, share your desire with people you trust to give you unbiased feedback. Weigh their feedback against the backdrop of your heart. Has the feedback you received from your friends convicted you of selfish intention and impure justification? The answers to these questions are meant to help you determine if you have a solid purpose for your request.

What we ask for is an indication of what we desire in our hearts. Our desires come from life experiences that have exposed us to things we have found desirable. But, and this is a big "but," just because you have been exposed to something does not mean it is worth pursuing. It takes discipline to separate your past experiences from your future desires. Mixing the two can result in you reliving your past and limiting your future.

It is worth noting that past experiences and exposures creates a false expectation of what is right for you. It is easy to find yourself frustrated with your life because it does not reflect your vision. This can be a result of you subconsciously *reliving your past in your present* without acknowledging your present is totally different from your past. Your maturity and perspective on life is totally different, yet you are completely reliant upon old experiences that have no place in the present. You owe it to yourself to update and sync your present with relevant experiences that contribute to helping you achieve what you desire. How do you do that?

1. Ask for what you want

2. Develop a plan to get what you want

3. Launch from where you are to make it happen

Ask for What You Want

People find themselves frustrated because they are asking for things that they want, but those desires do not align with their destiny and purpose in life. Unfortunately, this off-base thinking prevents people from experiencing fulfillment because what they want does not glorify God. Glorifying God is simply insuring, in the midst of success or failure, that your character and behavior is consistent with Scripture.

There will always be opportunities to cut corners and skip over the necessary steps to develop a sustainable foundation; however, a character consistent with Scripture does not support those efforts. In fact, the dissonance created by acting contrary to Scripture gets in the way of you receiving God's blessings. The dissonance between Scripture and your action presages a poor outcome to your efforts. Glorifying God is vital to any amount of success you expect to have. When your agenda is to glorify God, you will be very clear on what He has destined for you and what He has not. When your agenda is to glorify God, asking for what you desire becomes a whole lot easier. Your request is within the proper context of God's will for your life and cuts down on wasted time that can be applied to increasing the quality of your life.

The principles of asking for what you want

There are principles to asking for what you want. If you follow these principles, you will find out you will have something to leverage for your future. The principles for asking for what you want include knowing the purpose of your request, effective communication of a genuine request, talking to the right people, and knowing your value. This information grounds what you should be asking for and how to go about asking for what matters for your future.

1. Know the Purpose of Your Request

What is the purpose of your request? Do you know why you are asking for what you are asking for? Most people pursue things and positions in life without having a real reason for their pursuit. This generally is born out of jealousy and a desire to acquire what other people have. Pursuing what others have, assuming that you are not destined to replicate someone else's journey, puts you at odds with yourself. In essence, you are being dishonest with yourself if you are pursuing something solely because of what others have. Unfortunately, most people find themselves in this situation and are never happy with their lives. They feel their achievements are inauthentic, fake. The most critical aspect of the asking process is making sure that what you are asking for is aligned with your goals. Enjoying a future of promise depends on knowing how to filter what adds or detracts value to your journey.

Identifying the purpose of your request dismisses irrelevant and unnecessary opportunities that distract you from the path to your goal. People are often distracted by things that do not help them accomplish their goal, and as a result, waste time chasing after things that have no value. If you are called to be an architect, what sense does it make for you to strive for a career as an entertainer? The time you spend seeking to become an entertainer distracts you from perfecting your craft as an architect. It is like the child that was told to complete his chores by his parents but was distracted, along the way, by his video games. He never followed through with his chores and received the associated repercussions. If your goal is personal fulfillment, you do not want to be distracted by false "opportunities" along your path! To filter between opportunities that are valuable and those that are distractions, ask yourself how a given opportunity would help you reach your goal faster and more efficiently.

The scriptures are clear when it says a man has many plans but the purpose of God is what stands. People create all types of plans for whatever purpose they set for themselves, however, if people paid more attention to God and the plans He sets for them, they will have a better sense of what to avoid along their journey. They will have more wisdom to filter through the array of options that presents itself, whether in business or in personal relationships.

God has defined the parameters of what belongs to you. We tend to move ahead of God in response to our corporeal desires, which are steeped in selfishness and pride. Taking a step back to evaluate how God is moving in your life will save you years of wasted time. My father taught my brother and me to always acknowledge the traffic signs of God. He is very clear in giving us a green, yellow, or red light for every decision we are about to make.

2. *Communicate Effectively*

Assuming that you have ensured that your personal goals and desires are aligned with the focus and intent of your future, you have the tough task of sharing your goals and purpose with others; particularly those people that can help you achieve your goals. It is already hard enough to make a solid decision about your future, but to go beyond that and discuss your decision so it can actually come to fruition is an entirely different task. It can be stressful to share your vision with people because you become vulnerable to criticism over something that means a lot to you.

It may appear to be easier to not share your vision with other people to protect yourself. However, consider the fact that if you do not share this information, you forfeit the opportunity to strengthen your ability to defend what you believe in. When you do not share your thoughts and ideas with others, do not expect people to read your mind to give you the feedback you desire. It is almost like you are looking to get something for nothing. If it were that easy, how many of us would avoid the confrontation of explaining our dreams to people who will never understand them? If you remember the story of Joseph, he had a tough time properly explaining his dream to his brothers because he did not fully understand its application.

Truth be told, communicating what we want is not an easy task, nor should it be. There needs to be a difference between those who invest themselves in making things happen and those that wish for things to happen without working for it. Although feelings of fear can be overwhelming, there is no excuse for not communicating clearly what you need while at the same time expecting people to team with you in fulfilling these needs. It costs something to make things happen, and if the cost of getting what you need is opening your mouth and communicating, you must be willing to pay that price. Without clear communication, nothing happens.

3. Talk to the Right People

After overcoming the challenge of communicating what you are thinking, the next challenge you will have to overcome is making sure you communicate what you need to the right people. It is not enough to share what you are thinking, but you must make sure you put your request in the hands and minds of the person(s) that can do something about it. Scripture says, "In a multitude of counselors, wage war." Surround yourself with the right people to ensure you are waging the right war with the right strategy. Moving too fast with an unhealthy over anxiousness to share can cause you to link up with the wrong people and forfeit the opportunities that were designed for you.

4. Know Your Worth

What keeps most people from receiving what they want and deserve is that they do not know their worth. This can apply to finances as well as self-respect. Many people find it easy to avoid the conflict of discussing their worth and value to make others feel more comfortable with their perceptions. These perceptions cheapen who you are and what you bring to the table. Unfortunately, the person who suffers from all of this is you. You are valuable and are worth the fee you charge and the respect you deserve; however, the question you have to ask yourself is who is going to communicate your value to other people, if not you.

This is a difficult subject to discuss because most people are not comfortable with demanding their value. Do not expect others to pay the price of your perceived value without you asking for it. Do not expect others to know your worth inherently if you have not communicated it. If you want to receive what you believe is your value, you have to know your value, the reason you deserve to receive it, and how to communicate the complexity of your value in very simple terms. The moment you diminish your value or your worth, everyone that interacts with you will quickly do the same thing. They do this for their own benefit. This ultimately results in others making an insufficient investment in you and in your dreams.

Master your skills

As we talked about in the last section of the book, asking for what you want requires effective communication skills, talking to the right sources, knowing what you want, and finally knowing your value. All of these things working together in your favor prepare you to acquire exactly what you are looking for. In the book of Genesis, Jacob was dealing with a situation of near slavery and abuse from his father in law. When Laban finally offered Jacob an opportunity to be compensated for his fourteen years of labor, Laban wanted Jacob to name his price. For most people, this is a dream come true. To name your price is like giving someone a blank check, telling him to put any amount of money on it, and giving him the authority to cash the check.

I am sure Jacob must have felt some excitement by this offer, but regardless of what he asked for, Jacob knew his father-in-law could not afford his value and would not be in a position to gather the resources that would adequately compensate him. Jacob turned down the offer to name his price but instead decided to utilize a methodology to develop wealth from scratch.

People that have a wealth development mindset learn very quickly they can create their own wealth from the resources of others without putting their personal resources at risk. Napoleon Hill, an early twentieth century success writer, called it OPM – Other People's Money.

For Jacob, he had no choice but to create wealth from the resources of his father-in-law because he was cheated so badly and treated as a slave. The scriptures do not reference Jacob's compensation when he first agreed to work for Laban other than the two wives. There was no mention of any gain of cattle or servants, just two wives. For all intents and purposes, he gained two additional expenses with not enough income to support each woman and the children they would later bear for him.

Jacob had contributed to Laban's increase in wealth. Jacob knew that true wealth could only be gained from creating and receiving residual income. As you may know, residual income is income people receive that they do not have to work for or earn through labor. This is the type of income wealthy individuals understand.

Based on Jacob's experience, he could only create residual income with the trade he practiced for the past fourteen years, herding. As a byproduct of the time Jacob spent herding the cattle of his father-in-law, he also learned the science of animal husbandry. The fourteen years of hard labor in Laban's fields herding cattle taught Jacob the principles and concepts of managing an animal's diet and nutrition, fitness, and mating habits. He also learned the life cycles of grasses and flowers, which are important to the diet of cattle. He was able to utilize this information to develop a plan for financial wealth and stability that was far more rewarding than the buyout offer from his father-in-law.

It is difficult for a lot of people to see the brightness of their future because they do not see their everyday life experiences as a classroom for grooming the skills and abilities within themselves. Many people see their life experiences as a nuisance instead of a learning tool, unwelcome though it might be. Would you have viewed fourteen years of your life in virtual slavery as an investment in learning new skills and a new trade? Or would you have complained about the fourteen years as time wasted and grieved the hard labor that came along with it? Remember, the reason Jacob entered into this employment agreement was for his love and passion for Rachel. When everything else around you seems to offer nothing but frustration, you should be sustained by the love and passion for your goals to develop solutions to your challenges.

In the midst of Jacob's fourteen years of hard labor and slavery, the scriptures do not mention Laban's sons until Genesis 31. They appear to not be active participants in their father's business. This means Jacob was left to work by himself without any assistance or oversight from anyone.

It was general practice at that time for the sons, particularly the eldest son, to be active in the family business. Jacob was left alone to manage the cattle and to learn the business by trial and error. The lesson learned from this situation is that doing things by yourself is not always a bad thing. It can be frustrating because no one in his or her right mind wants to suffer beyond what is necessary. When doing our jobs, we all can appreciate assistance to lighten the load and reduce the amount of stress we take on. However, there are some insights we can learn from Jacob's situation that are applicable to the leverage experience. When you work by yourself, you should notice the following benefits:

- Creative freedom;

- Free opportunities to experiment without limitations;
- No distractions from lazy and uninterested people;
- No time constraints.

Working alone meant Jacob had uninterrupted access to all of the resources of his father-in-law. Although he was working harder than the sons of Laban, Jacob had the opportunity to be creative with how he fed the cattle. Creativity can result in efficiency in productivity and unexpected innovations. In Jacob's case, this resulted in the discovery of how to affect the coat or skin of newborn calves. This may seem simple and unimportant to you; it was clearly unimportant to Laban, but this discovery paid huge dividends to Jacob.

Hungry for success

In the midst of the fourteen years of near slavery, Jacob was hungry for success and for the destiny that was available to him. Evidence of this attitude was shown as early as his birth when he battled his twin brother to be born first to receive the family birthright as he exited their mother's womb. The traditions of that time gave the birthright to the oldest son. Although Jacob was not born first, he never gave up on acquiring the birthright. When his brother was hungry and wanted to eat some porridge, Jacob used his brother's need as an opportunity to barter for his brother's birthright, which he was able to acquire successfully.

Jacob solidified his claim to the family birthright by tricking his father into believing he was his brother Esau. As a result, Jacob received the family blessing from his father but had to quickly leave home for his uncle's house out of fear for his life for what he did. He left home with no money or safety. However, he did leave with the blessing of the first-born, which was a prophetic word of leadership and success in his lifetime. This situation brings us to why Jacob and his fourteen years of near slavery with Laban is significant to our understanding of why and how to leverage what is inside each of us to achieve our goals.

In addition to grabbing his brother's foot during birth and subsequently purchasing the birthright for soup, Jacob wrestled an angel until he was blessed. He did not give up easily; he wanted to ensure he was always in a position to receive what was destined for him.

By the time Jacob arrived at Laban's house, he was aware of his ability to achieve anything he put his mind to. After completing fourteen years of service, Jacob wanted to be released from his father-in-law so he could freely provide for his family and not depend upon Laban. A person that wants to be free and deal with the uncertainty that comes with entrepreneurship is confident in their ability to replace the loss of perceived "stable income" through employment.

As survivors of the financial collapse in the early 2000's, we know that no job, 401k, or ancillary benefits are safe and tomorrow is not promised. It is vital that you learn this lesson. Before you go out and start acting like or telling people that you do not need them anymore, be sure what you are saying is actually true. People tend to boast about what they are going to do before they actually do it. This is dangerous because unnecessary pressure is added upon them, as boastful individuals, to perform or face humiliation. Failure to perform is a sure way of losing the respect of people who once respected you.

If you do not have money, wealth, or credit, the trust of people in your word is what should last when everything else fails. Prove that you have the skills and the capability to do what you say you can do. The proverb says, "Do you see a man skillful in his work? He will stand before kings: he will not stand before obscure men." When you have mastered your skill, trade, or profession like Jacob, during his fourteen years of slavery and grunt labor, you can test out new ideas, be creative, develop efficiencies and consolidate all your knowledge. You will be powerful enough to command the attention of kings – people that have the power to make decisions that redound to your benefit.

A legacy of leverage

When you are brought before kings, a onetime payoff for your wisdom or skills is not enough to define your full value. Your value is not based on the immediate response you receive from people. The reality is that people know the value you bring to a situation and will often try to get your value at a bargain price. They may want to take advantage of what you have to offer without paying the expense that is associated with it. It is up to you to ensure you receive all of your value and structure an agreement that compensates you for all that you are worth. Do not allow people to take advantage of you.

Some Christians struggle with the issue of fair compensation. Some believe that being a Christian includes not demanding respect through fair market value in exchange for products or services. The teachings of Christ did not support this at all. As the Son of God, He continuously advocated for his disciples and admonished the Pharisees to respect Him and His divinity. If you are clear about whom you are and your associated value, you should demand that everyone around you respect this.

The African American community struggles with debt and the lack of generational wealth. There seems to be no understanding of their value or how to leverage what they have to create wealth and ongoing blessings for their families to enjoy. Unfortunately, African Americans tend to be responsive to life as opposed to proactive, anticipating life changes before they arise. This creates a rift between what they hope to achieve and what they actually achieve. African Americans tend to respond to their immediate desires as opposed to embracing patience and strategic decision-making. Subsequently, future generations do not benefit from the mistakes of their parents and continue the trend of bad spending habits, no savings, debt, no investments, and slavery through wage employment.

The passing of this generational curse is on display in ravaged communities all over America. Black children are born into poverty with little hope of overcoming these seemingly impossible odds. These children contribute to the high statistics of persons burdening the welfare system as opposed to being self-sufficient. I am aware that African Americans do not make up the majority of those benefiting from entitlements, but I also believe African Americans can gain self-dependence, and financial independence, if they leverage their skills and intellect. These words are meant as an encouragement for all African Americans, including me, to dig deep within themselves to learn how they can leverage all they possess to create a brighter future for themselves and their families.

The scriptures say a good man leaves an inheritance to his children's children. Increasingly, more people are living selfish lives and tending not to think about life beyond their immediate needs. This leaves many families lacking financial and emotional stability. Fewer families are focused on leaving a legacy for future generations. Although the memory of who we are will fade after we die, our legacy should at least have a chance to last long after we die through our long-term investment strategies. The only way to ensure you are establishing a solid legacy is to leverage your gifts and skills to create this legacy.

If the leaders of our families, mothers, fathers, and others with family leadership responsibilities do not embrace the importance of a legacy, they will pass on to another generation the normality of long-term lack. There is something to be learned about leveraging your gifts and skills to change your future. Doing so speaks to the tried-and-true statement, "The best is yet to come." Our children are at risk of not experiencing the spirit of this statement because we are not leaving them anything. It behooves us to work on leaving something of true value and substance to the next generation so they too can leverage their assets to access a prosperous future.

Getting good advice

When Jacob left home, his father pronounced a blessing over him that went as follows.

> *May God give you of the dew of heaven and of the fatness of the earth and plenty of grain and wine. Let people serve you, and nations bow down to you. Be lord over your brothers, and may your mother's sons bow down to you. Cursed be everyone who curses you, and blessed be everyone who blesses you! Genesis 27:28-29.*

A blessing like this is God's Word or advice delivered through the voice of others. In the passage above, Jacob receives critical advice as his blessing from his father. In addition, Isaac's words were prophetic. Let's take a closer look at Isaac's words.

"Dew of heaven, fatness of the earth, and plenty of grain and wine." In every endeavor in life, you should desire the best for yourself. God certainly desires the best for you. If you consider the words of Isaac, he is essentially releasing upon his son the resources of God's earth. To jump-start this release, there needs to be rain or dew that falls from the sky. The rainwater, as you may know, sparks the growth of food and provides life to organisms, the roots of which are deep under the soil. If God does not release the dew from the sky, there will be a famine. God initiates all the resources mentioned by Isaac. Without God, we cannot realize our potential and the blessings He has to offer us.

"Let people serve you and nations bow down to you." Having people bow down to you should not be your goal. The proper contextual thought should be becoming the chief servant of all. With greatness and success comes the responsibility of being good at what you do for the benefit of others. I am afraid there are too many young people growing up believing the world is at their beck and call and that the world is there to serve them. This attitude has led to the lack of respect for adults and figures of authority. To earn the right to have people bow down and serve you requires you to reach a plateau of success that has ultimately blessed others. "A diligent man in his business will stand before great men." Everyone must earn their way. There are no handouts in life, nor will there ever be.

"Be lord over your brothers and may your mother's sons bow down to you." The point of this proclamation is the older brother, the one with the blessing, can expect to receive the respect of his younger siblings. As in most families, the oldest sibling, particularly the brother, is looked up to for guidance and as a template for decisions.

"Cursed be everyone that curses you, and blessed be everyone that blesses you." Like the previous blessing, this statement is clear. If you have the opportunity to bless someone, do it. We interact with a lot of people every day and we are confronted with this dilemma quite often. There are times we do not realize our blessings are connected to how we treat people. We reap what we sow. The next time you express your feelings toward someone, be sure to determine how the projection of those feelings will return back to you.

Preparing for something new

Servants or employees are the by-products of the availability of work. When a leader or an employer has nothing to offer people, there is no need for servants or employees to help cultivate what does not exist. Proverbs 12:9 speaks to this truth. It says "Better to be lowly and have a servant than to play the great man and lack bread." In America, we have become accustomed to acting like and trying to become the Joneses but not spending enough time to develop the substance that supports this lifestyle. We tend to find greater pleasure in the effort of displaying wealth than putting in the work actually to gain it. These statements are not meant to demean the lives people choose to live; however, they speak to the importance of life prioritization that will, through focused, productive effort, lead to the fulfillment of your desires.

We want and anticipate things to happen in our lives, but unfortunately, we may not be prepared to handle the blessings that may be specifically meant for us. The Biblical example of this is the servant with one talent, a weight of silver. Unlike his counterparts, this person did nothing with the talent that was given to him. He did not trade it up for greater value, he did not use it as leverage to gain more talents, nor minimally, did he put it in the bank to at least gain interest and earn something on the money. The person with the one talent is a reflection of how most people treat their lives and the opportunities that are presented to them.

If you do not take opportunities seriously, you should not expect to experience all of their benefits. People that do this are the same people that will squander opportunities and blame others for their lack of success, while they watch other people take advantage of that same opportunity. It is important for you to see where you can improve your performance so you can be worthy of the opportunities that will be presented to you.

Prosperity requires a spirit of giving.

Success requires the capability of thinking beyond the immediate needs of right now. "Right-now thinking" is selfish and shortsighted. In turn, selfishness consumes any opportunity to succeed or experience success of any kind. Selfishness prevents prosperity. It is ironic, but the desire to accumulate more "stuff" in the here-and-now actually inhibits our substantive growth.

Selfish people do not give. They hold on to things and relationships that have outlived its usefulness. Selfish people also reduce their capacity to receive anything new. Giving helps each of us grow personally. Could it be that your blessings and the future you desire for yourself is merely one gift away? Giving suggests that you no longer have the capacity to keep what you have and need to give away what you currently have to make room for something new. The more you give, the quicker you realize the immediate opportunity to grow and develop.

The authentic "ask"

Many believers tend to ask for the wrong things. The things they ask for are not aligned with the trajectory of their lives. God says in James 4:3 this type of thinking results in people asking with the wrong intent. God does not bless us with things that do not rightly belong to us. 1 John 3:19-24 provides an interesting perspective on measuring how honest we are with what we are doing and what we are pursuing. If your heart condemns you as you pursue your desires, you will not be able to defend your action before God. If your heart does not condemn you, you can move forward knowing you have God's support.

All have sinned and come short of the glory of God. Our sinful ways create opportunities for us to operate outside of the will of God. If you desire to be aligned with the will of God concerning your future, you have to be willing to trust God to help you sort through the weeds of multiple opportunities and clearly identify the path for you. Operating outside of the will of God is dangerous and limits the amount of success you can hope to achieve. It is critical to make sure your expectations are in line with God and His commandments.

Managing your resources

The acquisition of wealth is not the end of your ability to be productive. The acquisition of wealth is a signal that you have achieved success in your area of focus. Wealth also means you are now managing assets, if deployed well, that will make more money. This concept is the same with blessings. When you are blessed, you are working to maintain your blessings. More importantly than that, you are now working to be blessed in a totally different way (earning interest). As you effectively manage your blessing, you quickly learn about all it has to offer. You become familiar with its benefits, its challenges, its pros and cons.

Receiving what you are asking for comes as a result of hard work on the right thing at the right time.

Hard work can be a turn-off for people who desire to become successful without putting in the necessary effort. The question you have to ask yourself is how badly you want what you are asking God for. How hard are you willing to work for it? How much are you willing to sacrifice to acquire it? These are some serious deep-seated questions to ask yourself before you start pursuing the thing you desire. Why waste so much time if you are not willing to work for it?

Many people are motivated by jealousy as opposed to the will of God and end up having unrealistic expectations for themselves. If you care how you spend your time, it must be equally important to you to know God's will for your future. Anything less will be a significant loss of your time.

Three

Formulate a Plan to Get What You Want

It is vital to realize a one-time payoff does not lead to you achieving your goals. It was not good enough for Jacob and it should not be good enough for you. Before you accept compensation in exchange for your value, there are several things to consider.

Know your worth

Your time is valuable and you should treat it like it is. The information you gain from how you spend your time is a valuable asset. Most people do not see the potential that is within themselves to start a business based on the skills they already possess. Most people behave as if their means to an end is associated with a specific salary. For your information, a salary is an amount of money paid to an employee that is often times not negotiable. Unfortunately, a salary is not an accurate depiction of your value. As a matter of fact, what job or place of employment can truly represent how valuable you are by the salary they pay you? Who wants to pay you a wage that is equal to your true value?

The truth is no one can truly afford you. You are priceless. No one can pay the price that you are worth. For Christians, we know this to be true because Jesus paid the price for our sins. Salvation opened the door for us to live life free from sin. If what I am saying is true, why do we waste our time trying to find someone to compensate us for our value? Despite all of the energy you put out, you will never find equal compensation for your value beyond what Jesus paid. If you naïvely continue to search for it, you will continuously find yourself disappointed. It is in your best interest to identify ways to create the value you believe you are worth.

Assign tasks to your time

Your value may be infinite but your time is not. When your time is allocated to a particular activity, you have to spend it wisely on activities you desire to master. Life experiences are meant to help you grow. But if you spend your time doing something not worth mastering, your time will be wasted. Time is a precious commodity that each human being has in a finite amount, and we are empowered by God to manage it.

The responsibility for allocating your time lies squarely on your shoulders. Even if you never become a CEO, a leader or an influential person, you will always have CEO power over your time and what you do with it. In addition, remember, time waits for no one. Before you know it, five to ten years will pass by and you will look back and wonder what you have done with your life in that time. If you know this will happen, and it will, it behooves you to plan out your time and what you will be doing with it. Assign activities to your time, assign resources to your time, and assign relationships to your time. You will end up appreciating this and your time will thank you. Learning and mastering this is equivalent to unlocking the secrets to success and wealth.

Master your trade or skill

Use your time to learn something new or achieve mastery over something you already do well. This simply equates to becoming educated. People are quick to equate education with college, but education is much broader than the parchment a diploma is written on. Education is learning a new activity or behavior that will equip you to accomplish a task. Education occurs more often than people realize. Some people are educated by life, some by experience, some by a teacher or mentor, and some in a classroom. Regardless of how you are educated, it is critical to know that education is the engine for true success.

If you are not willing to invest in your education, you are not willing to invest in your growth. You need education just as much as the next person. Your focus should not be to walk down the graduation aisle but to learn from someone that knows more than you about the subject matter you care about. When you know that you are educated about what you are doing, you have power; at least more power than you had before. You have more power to think, to perform at your best, and to be whomever you want to be because you now know how to function with your newfound knowledge.

Learn people

Not knowing people is like not knowing yourself. When you do not know people, you lose valuable opportunities to learn about who you are, what you like, what interests you, what annoys you, and what makes you happy. These key data points help you determine who other people are and how you should generally, and I mean generally, deal with them. What you learn about people should not be used as a lump sum measurement of everyone; rather, the principle of learning about people should be a principal practice in all your interactions.

The more you learn about people, the more equipped you are to guard against people that are not helpful to you during your growth period. Our exemplar, the Biblical Jacob, did not know his father-in-law Laban was scamming him. If Jacob knew this information, we can assume he would have made other arrangements with his father-in-law when he first arrived. The lesson that can be learned from this process is that learning about people and their intentions before you develop a relationship with them will save you a lot of trouble and heartache in the future.

Communicate clearly

If you cannot communicate clearly, you cannot enroll other people who could help you achieve your goals. I will admit, communicating can be difficult, particularly when it involves discussing topics that are sensitive to you. However, it is important to remember that if you do not share what you are feeling or thinking, no one will know how they can help you. Without communication, how would you know what other people are thinking? How can you be the best you can be for others if no one ever told you how to do that? How can they summon their best efforts on your behalf if you do not tell them what you need? Communication is a privilege God has given us and we have a responsibility to use it.

Before closing this chapter, I want to reiterate its message. You have to commit yourself to mastering your craft. Your craft is only valued at the price you set for it. No one can set that value for you and nor should they. When you allow people to set the price for your craft, you will never realize the benefits of being a master of your trade. This is why you hear so many wealth and personal improvement gurus and coaches tell their readers and clients to stop expecting their place of employment and the salary they receive to define their value. You will never be paid what you believe you are worth.

Think about it like this.

Many people across America are selling their homes. Many sellers are looking to sell their homes for what they think it is worth; however, the realities of the market dictate the value of the house and how much it will sell for. Your feelings cannot and will not ever affect the price of your home nor will they motivate a buyer to pay a price you feel they should pay. This is completely relevant to how you should view your life. People are not going to respond to how you feel and will not pay a price you feel they should pay. No more than they will pay the price that you set emotionally for your house will they pay what you feel you deserve for your time, skills, and expertise. They will pay a price for your services and what you have to offer based on the value they place on you.

If you come to terms with someone that is willing to buy your house at a price you set, great, but in most cases you will have to make some concessions that are dictated by your market. Only if you have a one-of-a-kind house will you be able to command a one-of-a-kind price. Similarly, if you want to be free of market forces for your time and talents, you need to develop one-of-a-kind talents. This is why mastering your craft is important. If you want to be worthy of a high value, prove it. Where are the results? Who have you affected? Who has benefited because of you? Prove your value by mastering your craft.

Four

Launching From Where You Are

You should be feeling good about the progress you have made thus far in the book because you have read through three powerful, life-changing sections of Leverage. As we move forward in this book, I want to explore the value of your plan and what it means to execute your plan. Your experience, as discussed in the previous sections, lays the groundwork for you to build on to strengthen the execution of your plan. Let's get right into it.

Words Matter

Before you begin to outline a business plan, you may have to adjust your self-talk. If no one ever told you before, I am going to tell you now...words have power! In fact, they have a lot of power. Their value is beyond what can be measured by money. That is why it is important to watch what you say and to whom you say it.

Words are deep-seated prophets of your soul. They tell whomever is listening what you are thinking, what you are feeling, and what you believe. People can draw near-exact conclusions of who you are and what you will do under stress. The Bible speaks explicitly about words, stating that life and death is in the power of the tongue. The tongue speaks the words that are deep inside our hearts. The words you use with your tongue disclose the intent of your heart, and as a result, have awesome power to make things happen - good or bad.

Words prophesy the direction in which you will go. The most crucial application of this statement is when you face your perceived darkest moment and feel defeat breathing down the back of your neck. What you say to yourself next becomes critically important to your victory. Saying the right words to encourage yourself in a difficult moment is easier said than done.

In the midst of confronting a challenge, the first thing you probably think about is not a prophetic word, but a quick ready microwave solution to provide immediate relief. As difficult as this may seem to be, you must build your stamina during difficult times to learn how to speak a prophetic word to yourself and to your situation. Below are some pointers to help you through this.

(1) After dealing with the initial challenge of your situation, find a set of words that speak to a positive outcome of that situation. If you are dealing with financial difficulty, speak to yourself about the solutions you will employ to solve that problem, write those

words down, organize the words into a formal plan, and execute that plan. If you have serious health concerns, speak the words of healing (better mobility, independence, no pain, etc). Write these words down, formalize these words into a plan that incorporates the directions of your doctor, and execute.

(2) Share your frustration with others and allow them to speak to and with you. Allow people to talk to you and share with you their perspectives on your situation. Most of what people say may be irrelevant to you because they do not know your situation in as much detail as you. However, the things they will say to you may have some positive impact on how you handle the situation going forward. As the saying goes, take the meat, leave the bones, and keep moving. This statement is meant to encourage you to listen better and find the value of what others have to offer you and leverage it to your advantage.

(3) Remove words from your vocabulary that can impede your progress. Regardless of the progress you

attempt to make, your choice of words has enough power to prevent you from overcoming sudden obstacles. When something hits you out of the blue, will your reaction move you toward a successful resolution? Or will your reaction be another obstacle in your path? People often sabotage their own prospects because of their choice of words. Honestly speaking, the choice of words we employ is a result of our thinking and how we perceive things. Not having the right perspective on things results in the misappropriation of energy into areas that do not require it.

(4) Stop hurting your feelings with the words you speak to yourself. Words have staying power and the ability to hurt deeply. The words we hear from others hurt deeply; also, the words we say to ourselves can hurt deeply. We often say negative, disconcerting things about ourselves, particularly when we do not meet our personal expectations. In most cases, we do not realize that we are saying things that will stunt our progress. Calling oneself stupid and crazy and dumb for making

mistakes is something that happens all too often. People tend to talk themselves out of trying again; out of encouraging themselves to confront the challenges that contribute to their failure. Words hurt. Words can hurt badly enough to create self-hate and self neglect.

The impact of words

I mentioned in the introduction to this section that before you write your plan, you have to learn to manage your self-talk. Negative self-talk inflicts deep wounds and can restrict your competitive advantage in life. Negative self-talk stunts growth. Below are some principles about words. Study these principles with the intent of building your internal strength to leverage what you have for affective life change.

(1) Words can hurt so badly that they can cause depression. Words run deep like the deepest ocean with no perceptible floor. The wrong words make it hard to manage the onslaught of the feelings they engender unless the receiver of these words has stable footing. For

Christians, our stable footing is on our faith in God and His reviving love through His son Jesus.

(2) Words have the power to make you feel better. When all hell is breaking loose in your life and you do not know where to turn next, the right words spoken at the right moment can make a situation turn around. Proverbs 25:11 says, "A word fitly spoken is like apples of gold in settings of silver." In order for words to have a positive impact, you need to imbue them with positivity and power.

(3) Words conjure up emotions you did not know existed. Sometimes, the words we hear and speak cause unexpected feelings and emotions to arise. Because of this, you need to prepare in advance an appropriate response to control these emotions.

(4) Words can make fear rear its ugly head. Fear is the embodiment of our worst nightmares and thoughts. Fear causes a paralysis of the mind and ankyloses our mind's agility. If you think you have what

it takes to do something great, just know that fear is the true enemy of greatness.

(5) Just as words can tear down the confident, words can embolden the fearful. The right words can pump up those that feel less than or unqualified for their pursuits. What if you had the right words to strengthen your ability to become whom you desire? What change would you see in yourself? How would you respond to that change? How much faster would you achieve your goals?

(6) The right words can provide vision to a visionless person. When the right words are spoken, it can provide the clearest view on how to get from point A to B.

(7) Words can limit or enhance how you view things, people, and information. Sometimes we can hear words that can cause us to think small-mindedly and reduce our ability to be creative and thoughtful. Sometimes words can build us up and make us see the Godliness within us. If starting or building a business,

family, career, etc. is on your agenda, you must seek the words that lift you up and broaden your vision, and avoid or discount the words that limit your vision and thought.

Putting it all together; leveraging where you are

Your perspective in life is controlled and impacted by the words you speak. Proverbs 12:18 says there are people that speak words like swords or piercings; but the tongue of the wise is health. If you reflect on the many times you have discouraged yourself from making good, strong decisions because of the words you spoke to yourself, you will begin to think of all of the great opportunities life has offered you that you have turned down or missed out on. Some of the words we speak to ourselves stab the air out of our dreams until we fall helplessly back to our current reality. Some of these words may include the following:

"This is too hard,"

"I have no one to support me,"

"This is taking too long,"

"If only I had this or that, I would be successful."

These words are dangerous to your growth and may be contributors that rob you of the life you desire.

You may be saying to yourself, "Why do my words matter to my being able to leverage where I am?" The truth is words inform your thinking and behavior. If, along your journey, you are not surrounded by words that speak to your future and the potential inside of you, you need to find the uplifting words that will carry you as if on eagles' wings. Think about the story of Joseph and his journey from being one of the youngest of his brothers to being number two in command of Egypt. Think of the words Joseph heard. First, he heard nothing but belittlement and rejection from his brothers. Next, Joseph was promoted to second in command in the house of Potiphar. We can assume Joseph heard words from Potiphar that spoke to his skill and success. Then, he heard the lies of Potiphar's wife and the false testimony of "witnesses." Finally, he heard the following words from Pharaoh: "Since God has shown you all of this, there is none so discerning and wise as you are." These are indeed powerful words, and are a culmination of Joseph's journey to greatness for the benefit of his family. It was also a fulfillment of the dream he dreamed when he was a young boy, which, when interpreted, said he would lord over his brothers and they would bow down to him.

Similarly Jacob, the second born of twins, exhibited certitude in his leadership because of Isaac's verbal blessing. When he and his brother were born, he came out holding his brother's ankle. We next found Jacob asking Esau for his birthright in exchange for soup. Esau responds to Jacob by saying, "what is my birthright to me? You can have it." We cannot blame Jacob for asking for it and for taking it when it was willingly given to him. The lesson to learn from the story of Jacob and Joseph is this: **Ask for what you desire, know why you** are asking for it, and leverage what you attain to make the life change you desire.

How many times do you think Jacob asked his brother for his birthright? How much time do you think Jacob spent watching his brother's work habits to determine the appropriate time to ask him for the birthright? How much time do you think Jacob spent perfecting the recipe of his soup to know that after consuming it, it would return to a man his strength after working hard? How much time do you think Jacob spent studying the value of the birthright and all that came with it? The answers to these questions contributed to Jacob's **asking for what he desired, knowing the purposes of his ask, and leveraging the birthright to make the life change he desired.**

The old adage, "be careful what you ask for, because you just may get it," applies in this situation. Both Jacob and Joseph knew why they were asking for such great things. Through vision and revelation, they knew undoubtedly they were able to manage the results of their request, grow their gifts, and leverage what they obtained for their advantage. I must point out here that neither Joseph nor Jacob knew the total value of their requests. Although Joseph knew his brothers would bow down to him, he did not know the fulfillment of his dream would come by way of managing Egypt through prosperity and famine. Jacob knew blessings would come from having the birthright but he did not know he would realize the blessings of the birthright while enslaved by his father-in-law.

The ability to plan is critical to leveraging where you are and what you have. As the saying goes, "if you fail to plan then you are planning to fail." Planning has to become a part of your repertoire if you expect to exercise your leverage. Strategic planning is the process of making clear decisions to reach goals. There is a direct connection between strategic planning and performance. As a result, strategic planning is often used to secure a competitive position. A strategic plan keeps costs low and maintains a distinct focus on the goals of the plan.

The absence of a plan threatens every opportunity for sustainability and provides a doorway to performance and infrastructure vulnerability.

Many do not achieve their goals because they do not have a documented strategy. Why do people refuse to plan? Simply put, strategic life planning is thwarted because people have low expectations of themselves. Some refuse to change, and for others, their relationships prevent them from doing what is necessary to improve their future.

Launch (Execute your plan)

After all of the hard work of planning, thinking, adjusting, overcoming challenges, and much more, it is now time for you to launch from where you are. Your thoughts and ideas are not meant to remain phantom objects on a piece of paper or an idea in your mind; rather, they are supposed to be shared with the world so that the world can benefit from what you have to offer. The human connection allows us to develop through learning from others as a part of our growth. This only happens when people decide to share their experiences. When people share, others work up the courage to investigate the potential of changing their behavior and ways of thinking to achieve their goals.

You do not always have to be a taker of the gifts and skills of others. You have every right to be a giver of gifts and abilities. An example of this is me writing and sharing this book with you. I am a strategist. I specialize in helping people develop personal strategies to resolve challenges that inhibit the success they desire. I do so by providing one-on-one coaching, teaching, training, and literature (books and articles). Although I am not meant or called to help everyone, I am called to help someone. Maybe that someone is you. Although I may not know you personally, I was meant to write this book for your benefit.

You are endowed with the same responsibility for the benefit of someone else, but this requires you to launch your gift and execute your plan. All of the struggles and challenges you have been through should not be in vain. Embrace the lessons you have learned from your experiences to make a difference in your life and the life of someone else. Do not be like those people that idly watch others move forward, criticize them with jealous intent and never execute a plan of their own to express their own gifts. Do something with your gifts. Execute your plan!

Five

My Testimony of Leverage

The leverage experience is more than reading about the basic principles of life change; it is also connecting to the experiences of others to make a difference in your life. Perhaps my story can be an example of what leverage can do for you. Before I start, you should know that leverage is a complete faith walk. Without faith, you will, in no way, put into action what is written in this book. The proof of your faith in God and what He can do for you is evident by the actions you decide to take or decide not to take. *"Faith without works is dead."*

My story of leverage begins when I entered college. I remember very distinctly catching public transportation to take my first class at Penn State University. As a matter of fact, taking public transportation from point A to point B was normal for me because I did not have a car.

As I walked down the hill to the first building, the parking lot was on my right hand side. The parking lot represented several things. First, it represented the beginning of my college career and second; it represented the biggest challenge I felt I had to overcome during my college career. The challenges the parking lot represented became the motivation that kept me going every time I walked past those cars on my way to class or to public transportation.

You must be asking yourself, what type of challenge could a parking lot ever pose to a college kid? Well, the challenge was not the parking lot itself, but what was in the parking lot. As a kid who grew up in a middle class home with a working mother and father, I was not used to seeing what I saw in the parking lot. What am I talking about? I am talking about the types of cars I saw in the parking lot. The parking lot I walked past every day was for student parking only. The types of cars I saw in the parking lot were newer and expensive. BMWs, Mercedes, and other types of nearly new vehicles were parked in a lot designated for student parking alone! This was shocking to me because in high school, my friends drove hoopdies (a car that was ugly but was able to go from point A to B). In high school, a hoopdie was way better than public transportation.

You may still be asking me, why was a parking lot full of new and expensive cars such a challenge to me. I never been the type of guy that drooled over cars, nor was I concerned with what others drove, mainly because at that time, I did not have anything to drive. What I later found out was these vehicles belonged to many of my classmates and they were the same age as me! The question I naturally asked next was how their parents could afford an extra vehicle, money to fill this vehicle up with gas, and of course, enough money to pay for insurance for a young driver.

Their parents were able to afford these cars and the associated expenses because they were either well-off managers of an organization or business owners. This was new for me too! I did not have many friends that had parents in this situation. Certainly, my family situation was not close to this. My father took care of our family well but was not an executive and not a business owner. Adding another car to the family's budget was not a realistic option. My mother assisted my father in providing for the family, but again, there was no real opportunity to increase the family budget for the sake of a car.

After discovering the background of my classmates, I realized something. I was not sure how I was going to compete with these same students for future job opportunities. I was not significantly connected. Nor was my father in a position to hire me into his company. Let me say, a lot of my classmates went on to work at large corporations and may have gotten there on their own merit, but many of them at least had a "back up plan" after college if the job search thing did not work out.

My immediate challenge was leveling the playing field so I could compete with my classmates, who I perceived to have a leg up on me. Their cars were symbols of the head start I was looking to close in the game of life. As a brand new college student, I did not know much about how to close this gap but I was determined to make up the difference.

As a young black student with no credible connections, no car, and no clear view of my future, I needed to start with what I had. I learned that employers, after four years of college, preferred to hire graduates that performed well in the classroom and had experience as an intern. Hence the importance of an internship, paid or unpaid, during your college years. As I embraced the idea of becoming an intern, I quickly decided that an internship would be the leveling of the playing field between my classmates and me. I needed to do something I knew they were not doing and were not prepared to do – obtain an internship as a freshman!

The journey to becoming a freshman intern was not easy for several reasons. Note these reasons are really legitimate, regardless of how hard I tried to negotiate them.

Reason 1: I had no college experience. Remember, I made the decision to intern early and often as a freshman. I barely got through several weeks of classes before I made this decision. This meant I was not battle-tested as a college student. I had not so much as taken a test, let alone survived my first pop quiz, turned in a report, dealt with a difficult professor, overcame the defeat of a poor grade, struggled with the physical toll of walking across campus in ten minutes with books in hand, confronted the discombobulation of group dynamics and the associated projects, and experienced the almost useless function of study groups with the one kid that sleeps through the entire session. These real experiences, and many more, define the college experience, and I had barely started that experience.

The other challenge I was not prepared for was balancing a full college course load and a work schedule that demanded intellectual engagement. My goal was not to work in retail while in college, although there is nothing wrong with that. The distinct difference between working in retail and working as an intern, depending on the type of internship, is the intellectual involvement that is needed to do well at the job, working through office politics, and determining how to leverage all that you learn in the classroom in a real world environment. I quickly learned that I needed some serious discipline to function as a full-time student and full-time intern. I was so focused on leveling the playing field with my peers that I committed myself to seeing this strategy through to the end.

Reason 2: I had no credible work experience. For a student, credible work experience can be developed in multiple ways.

- Class projects and assignments;
- Completion of a course in a specific subject area;
- Actual work experience, paid or unpaid.

As an incoming freshman, I had none of this experience. The experience I had coming into college was a brief stint as a camp counselor, a staffer at a local museum, and summers working with my grandfather as he ran his business. I certainly was aware of the importance of work and I believe I developed a solid work ethic with my limited experience; however, I could not say at that time my experience was worthy of an internship and the investment of a company. Although I could not justify pursuing an internship with my limited experience, I knew I needed to get one anyway so that I could build some experience and avoid being rejected by companies after graduation. As it turned out, the quantity and quality of my internships helped me meet my strategic goal of closing the gap!

Let me say the great ideas you come up with means nothing until you execute it. Further, these great ideas may not monetize the way you want them to for quite some time. This was also my experience.

The Office of Career Services on the college campus helps upperclassmen find internships and career opportunities. Although the idea of an internship as a freshman was a great one, I also quickly realized I would not be paid the same as an upper-class intern, if at all. So I had to decide: did I want the money or the experience. I decided the experience was more valuable.

My first experience as an intern was in the computer lab on the campus college in my second semester. I provided hardware and software support and was a customer service representative to students and faculty. This job became a long-term internship opportunity for me to build upon. This was a great start because I was an Information Technology (IT) major. I thought I could use what I learned in the classroom in the computer lab on campus.

Next came an internship at the Greater Philadelphia Hotel Association as a business management intern. I was responsible for planning summer projects, developing a database to house affiliate contact information, and providing minor PC support. Not bad for a freshman going into a sophomore year.

I worked at the Hotel Association three days a week. The wonderful thing about the college schedule is I was able to arrange the schedule of my courses in a way that suited me. I often took courses on two or three specific days during a set block of hours. My flexible college schedule allowed me to commit a significant amount of time to both a job and an internship. When I was not at the hotel association or in class, I was working at UPS from 6 p.m. – 9 p.m. It was OK money for a freshman and it kept my basic living expenses paid. It also did not hurt to live at home with my parents so I did not have to pay rent or utilities. The entire time I interned at the Hotel Association, I was not paid, but the experience and resume booster was worth every moment.

After the Hotel Association, I interned at Comcast Cable, the parent company of Xfinity. I worked in the Government Relations department. Another part of my strategy to close the gap was to diversify my experience to complement the technology skills I would learn in the classroom. Penn State's IT program promotes the idea that IT professionals should be able to understand the needs of the business and translate those needs into technology solutions that are easy to use. This was ingrained in me and deeply influenced the belief I held that every experience that gave me exposure to the business units outside of IT would help me become a more marketable IT professional when I graduated.

My internship with Comcast was unpaid. As I stated before, the lack of compensation did not deter me from pursuing the opportunities I wanted and needed. I maintained my computer lab job, which paid me, while I interned at Comcast to keep money in my pocket.

At Comcast, I led the planning for the public screening of a movie during African American History

Month, interacted with local government officials, and did some business writing. These diverse experiences opened more doors for me. Although these projects were not technical in nature, I learned some serious business skills and enhanced my ability to build relationships.

The Comcast internship was a great match with my IT knowledge. I found a way to blend both worlds as Penn State intended for its IT students. I encourage you to engage in experiences that differ from what you are trained to do because these experiences add value to your core functionality.

Before I left Comcast, I secured an IT internship with Peco Energy and Unisys. Peco, now a subsidiary of Exelon, is the major electricity service provider in Philadelphia. This was a big deal because I began to feel the need to actually practice my information technology skills in the real world. I wanted to use my experience with coding and project management to produce tangible results. At Peco I did some website design, developed project plans, and worked on process improvement projects. At Unisys I worked on system testing and integration. I should take the time to tell you how I arrived at Peco and Unisys.

There is a national non-profit organization by the name of INROADS. The mission of INROADS is to prepare minority youth for their professional careers in specific areas including information technology. This preparation included training and securing interviews with corporate partners that reserved internship positions for INROADS interns. For quite a while, I maintained a relationship with INROADS by attending their trainings and building relationships with the staff but it took me several years to secure my first INROADS internship and it was with Peco.

Being an INROADS intern was fun and educational. My time at INROADS reinforced the sense of leverage my parents instilled in me. I got to meet other young aspiring students like me, which was encouraging. After the Peco internship ended, I was back at square one with INROADS. I could not find an internship with any of their partner corporations. Nevertheless, I was fortunate to secure an internship with Unisys on my own.

Several weeks before I started, I found out Unisys used to have INROADS interns and decided to discontinue the partnership. I immediately asked the staff at INROADS to reach out to Unisys to continue the partnership as long as I was an intern there. I asked because I wanted the benefit of being an INROADS intern while interning at Unisys. Being an INROADS intern meant I could attend trainings and receive ongoing mentoring support of the INROADS staff. That mentoring support was important because I had access to black professionals that could relate to me in a way my white supervisors could not. After I made my request to have INROADS and Unisys partner, I found out how hard it was to make that happen and why Unisys discontinued the relationship.

INROADS charged each corporate partner thousands of dollars per intern. The company had to pay not only the INROADS partnership fee, but also, they had to pay the salary of the intern, give the intern a desk, computer, phone, etc. In some cases, some corporations had 15 or more interns. This cost did not include the cost of other interns outside of INROADS. After some wrangling, Unisys and INROADS came to terms and I got everything I needed and wanted. I had another great summer with INROADS and I had a great internship at Unisys to add to my growing resume.

Between the Peco and Unisys internship, I got a job at PEPP Philadelphia, a joint project between Penn State and the School District of Philadelphia to intervene in the early educational experience of promising but underprivileged students. This program ensured the academic success of these students through mentoring and tutoring. I started out as a tutor but ended up an underpaid program assistant. Working with my supervisor, with whom I still have a relationship, gave me so much real world exposure to running a nonprofit organization. But my greatest experience at this job was learning how to deal with rejection and the absence of job security. I was not fired from this job; I worked very hard to make myself indispensable. The problem was, and still is in corporate America, that the lie people spread about making yourself indispensable is still alive and well. The lie is if you are indispensable, you have greater job security.

You can do all you can to make yourself seem more valuable than you really are but there are two outcomes that will most likely plague you. First, you may be fired because you are in fact disposable. Second, you may not be promoted or utilized to your maximum abilities because the work you have taken on to prove your value has not advanced your skills, professional knowledge, or the bottom line of the company.

This does not mean some people do not break through and achieve success by making themselves indispensable, but, you, the reader of this book, should be clear that it does not always work that way. In many cases, I found out that this advice did not work for me.

The lesson here is to leverage all the skills you have to pick up whenever your career is interrupted. Your ability to leverage is, in most cases, all you have to make the progress you are aiming for.

After working as an intern for several years I had two more semester to go before I graduated. I got an internship with Gemplus, a company that specialized in digital security. This internship was in IT market research. I researched the smart card industry, developed standards to compare Gemplus products to competitors, and developed a database of current and emerging smart card technology. I learned how to research the IT market before the work of managing a project and developing systems began.

At Gemplus, I learned how to collect and analyze data to justify new IT projects and initiatives. As you can imagine, I was busy building a body of work that would benefit me at the time I needed it. In fact, the semester I worked at Gemplus was around the time I needed to cash in all of my internship chips for the grand prize.

I wanted to work in IT full time. After completing all of these internships, I knew there had to be a dramatic ending to all of my hard work. I would not accept a negative result after all of the hard work I put in. When I entered my senior year of college, I mustered up all of the experience I gained over the previous three years to put together a targeted effort for a job in IT. The difference between my pursuit of a full time employment opportunity and an internship was the stiffer competition for fewer opportunities. As I started this journey, I felt really confident I would find something, perhaps as quickly as I had always found my other jobs and internships.

The name of the game at that time was to secure a job that started right after I graduated. For the college seniors that are reading this book, you probably already know the importance of establishing opportunities for yourself well in advance of graduation. I interviewed at several well-known companies. I felt I could use my past internship experience to create a difference between me and my unknown competition.

Along the way, I organized a bus trip to a job fair that was three hours away from my school, in hopes of finding and landing an opportunity. I spruced up the language on my resume to ensure that I was an attractive hire. I was working hard in my senior year to leverage all my assets to make a difference in my life and to level the playing field with my college peers who seemingly had more opportunities then I did.

Despite all of my hard work I did not find a job opportunity. I was disappointed and frustrated. I worked hard for three years finding job opportunities as an intern, working for free, working menial jobs to keep money in my pocket, going to school, involving myself in extracurricular activities, and I still did not land a job. The great job I was looking for at the end of my senior year was supposed to be the bow on top of the hard work I put in. And the disappointing thing about all of this was my peers were looking at me wondering what I was going to do to capitalize on all of this so-called hard work. No doubt there were so many people that were jealous of me, laughing at me, talking about me; believing I put myself out there too much. I started to wonder if I set too high expectations of myself and bit off more than I could chew.

The shock of my life came one day when I was in the gym playing basketball with friends. I got an email with a plane ticket attached to fly out to Hartford, Connecticut for a job interview with Aetna the insurance company. Aetna had a leadership development program that hired recent college graduates from diverse academic disciplines and put them through a training program to prepare these young emerging professionals to take a leadership role in various departments. I was shocked by this email for many reasons.

I do not remember applying to Aetna for a job opportunity. I did not know how they got my resume. I cannot figure it out to this day. I asked around to different friends and people with whom I had networked to see if they gave my resume to somebody. I found no answers. While I was investigating how my resume got to Aetna, I told my parents what happened and they were shocked as much as I was. It was late 2004 and very late in the process of job hunting for many college students. I was nervous, but I flew out to Hartford to see what was going to happen. I was not going to let this opportunity pass me by.

After I got back to Philadelphia, several weeks went by and I did not hear anything. I thought I did well during the interview process but I was still apprehensive about it, because of the rough time that I had with previous interviews. I started think I was not going to get the job. I began to think to myself, "Let me take a few weeks off from this process before I get back on the grind looking for a job." Suddenly, during a *riveting* game of table tennis, I received a phone call from an Aetna representative telling me I got the job, and that I was accepted into the IT leadership program. This was the most desirable program for recent college graduates in my area of study. She also told me what my salary would be.

At this point I do not think the salary is important to disclose to you, but what I will say about the salary is that it was very gratifying. That salary represented all the hard work I put in as an unpaid intern, as a lowly hourly rate intern and as a person who was working my way through college. My salary made me the highest-paid graduate of my graduating class. This means I was paid more than my peers, who had started out with those BMWs, Mercedes, and newer cars in that student parking lot four years prior. I was happy, I was satisfied, I was floored by the passion of my past and my excitement about my future.

Taking stock of this accomplishment, I was excited for myself and for all the challenges I overcame and the successes I achieved. My peers looked at me wondering how, why, what, where, when.

At this point I want to note one important fact about this entire book of leverage and even in my story of leverage. God is central to everything! This is not a cliché statement. I am saying this to make a broader point. The Bible says in James 2:17 – 18 that we express our faith in God and what God has promised to us by the work we do. This simply means that the faith I have in God is justified by the amount of work I put in to what I believe Him for. I believed if I worked hard and stayed committed to the plan and strategy I came up with on my first days of college, I would receive the blessings He promised me. He promised that I would be the head and not the tail. He promised I would be above and not beneath. He promised I would be blessed in my coming in and my going out. It is all in His Word. There is so much in the Word of God to obey and believe in. There are principles of life management and success that are in the Scriptures that can be gleaned if the reader just takes the time to read, process, and obey the Word. This was my core belief in college.

The last portion of my leverage story is about overcoming known barriers. For me it was the career services department of my school. You should know that it is important to work with the career services department of your school, if you are in college or trade school. But you also should know that the services they provide are geared to upperclassman (juniors and seniors). If you are like me and you have an interest in taking control of your career and your future at an earlier stage and with little resources, you should really pay close attention to my story. The central point of my story was my own desire to make things happen for myself. And there were a lot of things I had to do by myself and for myself without the assistance of the career services department.

If you remember, I said I put together a bus trip for students from my campus to meet a large number of employers who went to the main campus to do their recruiting. The campus I attended was small but was a part of a greater network of the larger college of Penn State University. At the time I gained awareness of this very popular and somewhat successful career fair. I managed to influence the career services department and student services department to fund a bus trip to this location which was three hours away. This was a big deal. No one did any such thing of this magnitude before. No students showed interest in the career fair at the main campus, so why did student services have to show any interest in creating such a trip? I had to lobby like a mad man to garner the funds from the school to get this trip paid for. After getting this trip paid for by the school only a handful of students showed up. Yes, only four or five students showed up. I would imagine that the school was not happy with this turnout, after they committed to paying the bill for the entire trip. Regardless of who financed the trip, I was a trailblazer. I was hungry. I needed to control my future by any means necessary. I needed this trip to happen because in my senior year, I still did not have a car. How else would I get to the career fair?

It was all about initiative. It was all about belief. It was all about the ability of faith the size of a mustard seed to move my mountains. It was not mysticism, but it was faith and commitment that started me on a journey that my privileged classmates envied. I leveraged everything within me and within my control to produce meaningful results.

In closing this book I want to leave you with a clear message. Leverage is all about what you make it out to be. You have everything you need inside of you - within you - to make a difference in the world if you use it. You have experience gained through the decisions you have made. Regardless of your socioeconomic background, you have everything you need to succeed. As my dad said to me over the years, "nobody can hold you back except yourself. You are your own worst enemy: you just have to know that and overcome this particular enemy." Leverage your assets, leverage your experiences, leverage the resources available to you and watch things change in your life.

One of the saddest moments in my life was working with public housing residents and watching them limit themselves. Many affordable housing communities abut well-to-do neighborhoods and are accessible to resources in a great city like Philadelphia, but the residents never set foot off of the premises. It is their mindset. It is all about the mind. Leverage is all about your mind.

> If you see something that you do not like in your life; fix it.

> If you see something that you do not want in your life; get rid of it.

> If you see something that you want in life; go get it.

I am not encouraging you to do something illegal or ill-advised, but this is an encouragement to get up and leverage what you have and work for what you want to make a difference in your life. If Jacob could leverage what he had to dramatically transform his life, you can do it too. If I can leverage what I had in my life to make a difference, you can do it too. HONOR THE GIFT GOD GAVE YOU BY TAKING ADVANTAGE OF EVERY OPPORTUNITY LIFE PRESENTS YOU. USE YOUR LEVERAGE!

Six

How to Develop a Leverage Action Plan

You have made it through the book! Congratulations. So you are asking yourself, how can you develop an action plan that will help you execute the ideas you have. Below are some thoughts on how to develop a solid action plan.

1. Understand your goals and their alignment with your vision.

2. Honestly assess your commitment to your goals.

3. Document your plan to reach your goals.

4. Determine how you are going to check on your progress.

5. Share your plan with someone that will hold you accountable and discuss methods of accountability.

Commentary on developing your leverage plan

Developing a leverage plan starts with gathering good, solid information that will lead to a desired outcome. Before you get started, simply state your personal mission. What are you looking to accomplish? This is the definition of your entire purpose and existence. Your personal mission notifies every one of your intentions. It speaks loudly and clearly to your expectations and your future behavior. It defines your thoughts. It encapsulates your agenda.

What are your goals? If you do not have goals that clearly identify how you are going to achieve your mission, you will be prone to making decisions that are not likely to lead you down the path you need to travel. You will need to refer to these goals often along your journey because the details of executing these goals sometimes obscure the original purpose of why you are doing what you are doing. You will be at risk of losing the vision of the forest while you are inventorying the trees. These reminders keep you on track and unfazed by distractions.

When you clarify your commitment level toward the goals you have identified, it puts into perspective where you will likely appropriate your energy and resources. One of the worst feelings to have is investing your resources in an idea and plan of action to which you are not fully committed. This creates dissonance between your heart, mind, and behavior. As a result, your will resources will gravitate to one side or the other or they will be forced to spread themselves too thin across all these competing concerns. As you evaluate your commitment level to the goals and ideas you have listed, you will be able to make a final determination of where you will invest the majority of your resources, both emotional and financial.

Once you narrow your ideas and choices, you must begin the process of discovering how to achieve the goal(s) you will pursue. This, quite frankly, is one of the most grueling things about this plan because you are forced to go beyond the semantics of emotional thinking and to research information to substantiate your reasoning. One of the reasons businesses, relationships, and partnerships fail is because people make assumptions that have no basis in fact. They subject themselves to the instability of assumptions written in thin air while hoping things turn out in their favor. Things do not turn out the way you want them to without the implementation of a plan that dictates the outcome. Your focus should be on developing a strong plan with substance and grounded facts. This will drive targeted outcomes. If the assumptions of your plan ignore the need for sound information and forward-moving action steps, you will be wasting your time.

The fun and hard part of this process is assessing how you are doing. When you check where you are on the trajectory of your plan, you will be able to view how far you have come since you started executing it. In addition, by viewing your progress, you can evaluate your current position and make adjustments, if necessary. Even if you feel it is embarrassing to discover you have not made the expected progress you planned for, you will be able to make corrections to the things that are not working so you can change the trajectory of your plan. This time and process has always proven to be an invaluable asset to successful people.

Finally, you will always need to have someone who will keep you honest about your plan. An accountability partner helps you remember what is important and why you are making sacrifices. The truth is the distractions of life can push you off course even if you have the best of intentions. Accountability partners help you remember your mission and your goals.

Seven

Works Cited

Al-Shammari, Hussam A., and Raef T. Hussein. "Strategic planning in emergent market organizations: empirical investigation." International Journal of Commerce and Management 18, no. 1 (2008): 47-59.

Carter, Hayley. "Strategic planning reborn." Work Study 48, no. 2 (1999): 46-48.

Desai, Ashay B. "Does strategic planning create value? The stock market's belief." Management Decision 38, no. 10 (2000): 685-693.

Harrison, E. Frank. "Strategic planning maturities." Management decision 33, no. 2 (1995): 48-55.

Pugh, Jonathan, and L. Jay Bourgeois III. ""Doing" strategy." Journal of Strategy and Management 4, no. 2 (2011): 172-179.

Schroeder, Roger G., Kimberly A. Bates, and Mikko A. Junttila. "A resource-based view of manufacturing strategy and the relationship to manufacturing performance." Strategic management journal 23, no. 2 (2002): 105-117.